Puppy Training
Step by Step Guide

With
Sarah Maisey

Dog-trainer.co

Important Notes

1. Even though your puppy is not fully vaccinated to mix with other dogs or to walk on the ground, take your puppy to as many places as possible (in the car, to a playground, cafes, shops etc) this allows the puppy to get used to smells, sights and sounds.
2. Don't allow puppy to have too many rooms at first, going somewhere completely different, on his own without siblings or mum can be very traumatic for a young puppy.
3. Ask the breeder for a toy a teddy or blanket, which has been in the whelping box, so when you are not around puppy still feels safe and can smell mum and siblings.
4. Crate train your puppy from day 1. Puppies are cute and cuddly but they do take up a lot of time and energy. If they are crate trained they will feel safe and secure. If you cover your crate with blankets (leaving one door uncovered) they will love it, as dogs are den animals. Crates should be used at night and if you leave puppy home alone. If you feed your pups dinner in his crate he will associate his crate as a good place to be. During the day you can leave the door open so he can come and go as he pleases.
5. The most urgent priority is to socialize your puppy to a wide variety of people, especially children, men, and strangers, before he is twelve weeks old. Well-socialized puppies grow up to be wonderful companions, whereas antisocial dogs are difficult, time-consuming, and potentially dangerous.
6. If you are home with puppy all day, all the time you can create separation anxiety. So leave pup alone in his crate for short 5 minute sessions at first and increase the time over a few weeks. It's best not to leave puppy for more than 2 hours.

7. Well-socialized puppies grow up to be wonderful companions, whereas antisocial dogs are difficult, time-consuming, and potentially dangerous.
8. Do not teach your puppy 'Paw' or 'high fiver'. As this is all they will offer instead of what you need to teach them.
9. Microchip – when you purchase your pup he should by law be micro chipped by the breeder, if not get it done.
10. Id tags for your dog's collar are also required by law and MUST have all the information required Your surname, if your surname sounds like a dogs' name like mine Maisey you can add Mrs or Mr in front, your house name or number, your postcode and a telephone number, it's a good idea to have a mobile number because if your pup is out and about alone, you maybe out looking for him.

Dog waste - All dog owners have a legal duty to clean up dog faeces immediately after their animal fouls a public place. Dog mess laws do not allow the excuse of **'not noticing'** that the canine has foul, dog poop can carry all sorts of nasty bacteria and parasites which includes the following:

- Hookworm
- Roundworm
- Giardia
- Lung worm

It is an offence not to pick up your dog poo and to dispose of it in a sanitary way which means you could be in for a hefty fine if you fail to do so.

If a dog sitter or walker regularly takes your pet out for their daily walks, you have to make sure they too pick up any poop during their walks which means making sure there are plenty of bags for them to use. The best place to leave the bags is next to your dog's lead, like this nobody will forget to take any with them when they go out for their daily walks. Owners can be issued with a fixed penalty notice of up to £100 for not complying with regulations.

11. Always have dog waste bags on you as you could be fined if you are walking your dog without them.
12. Alabama rot, otherwise known as Cutaneous and Renal Glomerular Vasculopathy (CRGV), is a disease affecting dogs by causing damage to the skin and kidney's blood vessels. When walking your dog in the countryside, make sure you wash off any mud from your dog's paws, belly and chest. If you do notice any scabs on your dog, visit your vet to get it check.

I have used him and her, he and she to refer to your puppy in this booklet.

Willing Compliance
• When a puppy approaches promptly and happily, it is a sure sign that he is people-friendly.
•Sitting and lying down in close proximity to people further shows that your dog likes them. Using food lures and rewards in training is the best possible way to teach your dog to like children and strangers.
• A puppy that has been taught by a range of people to lie down and roll over will have learned to show friendly appeasement and deference upon request.
• Most important, by coming, sitting, lying down, and rolling over on request, your dog shows respect for the person issuing instructions. This is especially important with children. When children lure/reward train, they issue requests (commands), and the dog happily and voluntarily complies (obeys). And when it comes to dogs and children, happy and voluntary compliance is the only type of compliance that is effective and safe.

Commands
How to train puppies
Let's just take a moment to think about how we are going to train your pup and what she's thinking.

To start with we need to lure the pup into position, once the pup is in the desired position we reward with the treat (kibble) this reward MUST come in as the pup has completed the desired position, timing is everything. We then need to do several repetitions. At least 5 repetitions so the pup starts to learn what we are asking her to do, but no more than 10 repetitions as the pup will only get bored and we don't want that. Once the pup gets the hang of the command then introduce the 'CUE' sit, down, etc.

Continue to use the lure, treat and cue, eventually the cue will come before the action. Everyone in the household will need to train the pup, training needs to be done little and often everyday by everyone. Try and work these commands into your daily routine this way the pup won't know he's being trained and you won't know your training your pup.

DO NOT push on your dogs' bottom or pull the legs to get her into a down position. By doing this the pup has learnt **nothing** because you have done the work or exercise for her. Patients, calmness and being consistent will get you what you want.

Puppies remember the last thing they have done, so if you have some really nice heel work then you ask for a sit you've just rewarded the sit.

Dogs are **location sensitive** this means puppy might do a sit, a down a recall etc in the house or the garden but when you get to the park you need to retrain your puppy because of the distraction you will also need to take high value treats with you too.

So, you might want your pup to sit and wait until you put the pups' dinner on the floor, sit and wait at curbs, settle down when you eat dinner/lunch etc.

Try and get into the habit of only commanding ONCE, if you use a cue 10 times, say to get your dog to sit, so 'sit, sit, sit etc. you are diluting that command. Until that cue actually means nothing to the pup. If you for example want your pup to sit, first use his name to get her attention the say 'sit' if pup doesn't do it straight away just wait a few seconds and you will find it might take a bit of time but your pup will sit. If the pup gets distracted you may need to re-command but count to 10 before using the pups name then sit.
It's also a very good idea to use hand signals, these may be similar to your lure signal as your pup will read your body language.
I recommend you use kibble for training in the home and garden, but when it comes to puppy class and going out for walks you will find that the kibble is not working as a reward so I suggest you use something a bit more high value such as cocktail sausage, ham, chicken etc.

Always finish on a high. If you start an exercise and maybe your pup has done the exercise perfectly on the second go, finish it there do not be tempted to have another go. By having another go what you are saying to your puppy is 'that wasn't good enough lets do it again'. This will also knock her confidence.

Puppy play is all important.
Play is essential if a puppy is to learn the social relevance of the vast jumble of behaviours.
In a sense, play enables a pup to learn what he can get away with. What you need to do is teach your puppy the rules of the game. And the more rules he learns in puppy hood, the safer he will be as an adult dog.

Puppy barking and growling are quite normal and acceptable, just as long as you can stop the noise when you wish. Stopping an eight-week-old puppy from barking or growling is pretty easy. Be still yourself, so the puppy may calm down more easily. Say, "Puppy, Shush!" and waggle a food treat in front of his nose. Say, "Good dog," and offer the treat when the pup eventually shushes. Similarly, tug-of-war is a normal and acceptable game, just as long as your pup never initiates the game and you can get the pup to release the object and sit at any time. Both are easy rules to teach to an eight-week-old puppy. When playing tug-of-war, instruct your puppy to release the object and sit at least every minute. Periodically stop tugging, say, "Thank you," and waggle a food treat in front of his nose. When the puppy releases the object to sniff the treat, praise him, and ask him to sit. When he sits, praise him profusely, offer the food treat, and then resume the game. **Important you start the play and you finish the play. Have a special toy that only comes out when you want to play with your pup like a tuggy rope or soft toy.**

Learning Bite Inhibition (By Four-and-a-Half Months of Age)

Puppies bite—and thank goodness they do. Puppy biting is normal, natural, and necessary puppy behaviour. Puppy play biting is the means by which dogs develop bite inhibition and a soft mouth. The more your puppy bites and receives appropriate feedback, the safer his jaws will be in adulthood. It is the puppy that does not mouth and bite as a youngster whose adult bites are more likely to cause serious damage. The puppy's penchant for biting results in numerous play bites. Although his needle-sharp teeth make them painful, his weak jaws seldom cause serious harm. The developing puppy should learn that his bites can hurt long before he develops jaws strong enough to inflict injury. The greater the pup's opportunity to play-bite with people, other dogs, and other animals, the better his bite inhibition will be as an adult. For puppies that do not grow up with the benefit of regular interaction with other dogs and other animals, the responsibility of teaching bite inhibition lies with the owner.

Puppies need to stay with their siblings and mother until they are 8 weeks plus. Play fighting with their siblings teaches them how hard is too hard.

Good Bite Inhibition

Good bite inhibition does not mean that your dog will never snap, lunge, nip, or bite. Good bite inhibition means that should the dog snap and lunge, his teeth will seldom make skin contact and should the dog's teeth ever make skin contact, the inhibited "bite" will cause little, if any, damage.

Decreasing the Frequency of Mouthing

Once your puppy has been taught to mouth gently, it is time to reduce the frequency of mouthing. Your pup must learn that mouthing is okay, but he must stop when requested. Why? Because it is inconvenient to drink a cup of tea or to answer the telephone with fifty pounds of wriggling pup dangling from your wrist. That's why.

It is better to first teach "Off" using food as both a distraction and a reward. The deal is this: once I say "Off," if you don't touch the food treat in my hand for just one second, I'll say, "Take it" and you can have it. Once your pup has mastered this simple task, up the ante to two or three seconds of non-contact, and then to five, eight, twelve, twenty, and so on. Count out the seconds and praise the dog with each second: "Good dog one, good dog two, good dog three," and so forth. If the pup touches the treat before you are ready to give it, simply start the count from zero again. Your pup quickly learns that once you say "Off," he can not have the treat until he has not touched it, for, say, eight seconds, so the quickest way to get the treat is not to touch it for the first eight seconds.

In addition, regular hand feeding during this exercise encourages your pup's soft mouth. Once your pup understands the "Off" request, use food as a lure and a reward to teach it to let go when mouthing. Say, "Off" and waggle some food as a lure to entice your pup to let go and sit. Then praise the pup and give the food as a reward when he does so. The main point of this exercise is to practice stopping the pup from mouthing, and so each time your puppy obediently ceases and desists, resume playing once more. Stop and start the session many times over. Also, since the puppy wants to mouth, the best reward for stopping mouthing is to allow him to mouth again. When you decide to stop the mouthing session altogether, say, "Off" and then offer your puppy a Kong stuffed with kibble.

Teething
Puppy Teething

Puppies usually have their entire 'baby' (aka *'deciduous'* or *'milk'* teeth) in place by the time they're about 8 weeks old. They only have a full set of these tiny, razor-sharp teeth for about a month. The teething stage usually starts at around the 12 - 14 week mark. Sometimes a drop or smear of blood on a toy or bone is the first sign that you have a teething puppy. Some pups seem to find teething uncomfortable, others don't even notice it's happening. however YOU will probably notice as a teething puppy has a compulsion to chew on everything he can find. The pressure that chewing puts on his gums helps him feel better, and it also encourages his baby teeth to fall out, allowing the adult ones to grow in.

Chewing plays an important role in your pup's dental development.

We all know that a teething baby can be uncomfortable and miserable, and that soothing his gums and giving him the right kind of 'teething toys' can help make him feel better. Now not ALL puppies get upset or distressed when they're teething.

Some will find this stage painful, but most of these seem to be uncomfortable more than in real pain - although the occasional pup may whimper or seem to be actually hurting. You don't need to *do* anything to 'help' the loose or wobbly puppy teeth to come out, so don't fiddle with them.

What you can do to help (and *should* do) is make sure your puppy has plenty of safe, sturdy chew toys to play with.

These will help soothe his sore gums, satisfy his urge to chew, and help protect your furniture, shoes and home from his determined chewing efforts.

Of course, puppies are perfectly happy to chew anything that comes anywhere near their mouths, and often the forbidden items seem oh, so much more *interesting* than the ones in his toy box.

So, during these months you're going to need to be extra vigilant about discouraging 'inappropriate' chewing habits or you could find that your home furnishings will take a beating!

Although they will come through the puppy teething stage eventually - even without any assistance from their owners - most will benefit from a little extra puppy teething help. I find a Kong stuffed with wet kibble and treat a great relief on their gums especially if frozen. So puppy's breakfast frozen in a Kong is a huge relief for your pup, so you may need to get two!

Adolescence is coming!

By now you're probably quite exhausted by your puppy raising efforts. Hopefully, though, you are justifiably proud of your well-mannered, well-behaved, highly socialized dog with dependable bite inhibition. The challenge now is to maintain your dog's stellar qualities. The prime purpose of puppy husbandry is to produce a friendly, confident, and biddable pup, so that you can face the behaviour and training challenges of your dog's adolescence, and your dog can deal with the immense social upheaval that dogs, especially males, face as they navigate adolescence. It is much easier to approach doggy adolescence with an already socialized and well-trained dog. However, maintaining your dog's socialization and training through his adolescence can be tricky if you don't know what to expect and how to deal with it.

Changes during Doggy Adolescence

Behaviour is always changing, sometimes for the better, sometimes for the worse. Things will continue to improve if you continue working with your adolescent dog, but they will definitely get worse if you don't. Both behaviour and temperament will tend to stabilize, for better or worse, as your dog matures around his second birthday for small dogs or third birthday for large dogs. But until then, if you don't keep on top of things, there can be precipitous and catastrophic changes in your dog's temperament and manners.

Even when your dog reaches maturity, you should always be on the alert for the emergence of unwanted behaviours or traits, which you must quickly nip in the bud before they become hard-to-break habits. A dog's adolescence is the time when everything starts to fall apart, unless you make a concerted effort to see it through to the stability of adulthood. Your dog's adolescence is a critical time. Ignore your dog's education now and you will soon find yourself living with an ill-mannered, under-socialized, hyperactive animal.

Here are some things to watch for:
Household etiquette may deteriorate over time, especially if you start taking your dog's housetraining and other good behaviour for granted. But if you taught your pup well in his earlier months, the drift in household etiquette will be slow until your dog reaches his sunset years, when housetraining especially tends to suffer.
Basic manners may take a sharp dive when puppy collides with adolescence. Lure/reward training your puppy was easy: you taught your pup to eagerly come, follow, sit, lie down, stand still, roll over, and look up to you with unwavering attention and respect.

But now your dog is developing adult doggy interests, such as investigating other dogs' rear ends, sniffing urine and faeces on the grass, rolling in unidentifiable smelly stuff, and chasing squirrels. Your dog's interests may quickly become distractions to training, so that your dog will continue sniffing another dog's rear end rather than come running when called. (What a scary thought, that your dog would prefer another dog's rear end to you!) All of a sudden he won't come, won't sit, won't settle down and stay, but instead jumps up, pulls on-leash, and becomes hyperactive.

Socialization often heads downhill during adolescence, sometimes surprisingly precipitously. As they get older, dogs have fewer opportunities to meet unfamiliar people and dogs. Puppy classes and parties are often a thing of the past and most owners have established a set routine by the time their dog is five or six months old.

At home, the dog interacts with the same familiar friends and family, and is walked, if at all, on the same route to the same dog park, where they encounter the same old people and the same old dogs. Consequently, many adolescent dogs become progressively dissocialized toward unfamiliar people and dogs until eventually they become intolerant of all but a small inner circle of friends. If your adolescent dog does not get out and about regularly and few unfamiliar people come to the house, his delocalization may be alarmingly rapid.

At five months your dog was a social butterfly with nothing but wiggles and wags when greeting people, but by eight months of age he has become defensive and lacking in confidence: he barks and backs off, or he snaps and lunges with hackles raised. A previously friendly adolescent dog might suddenly and without much warning be spooked by a household guest. Puppy socialization was a prelude to your safe and enjoyable continued socialization of your adolescent dog. However, your adolescent dog must continue meeting unfamiliar people regularly, otherwise he will progressively dissocialize. Similarly, successful adolescent socialization makes it possible for you to safely and enjoyably continue to socialize your adult dog. Socialization is an on ongoing process.

A dog's first adolescent fight often marks the beginning of the end of his socialization with other dogs. Again, this is especially true for very small and very large dogs. Owners of small dogs are understandably concerned about their dog's safety and may be disinclined to allow their dogs to run with the big dogs. Here is where socialization starts down hill and the small dog becomes increasingly snappy and scrappy. Similarly, owners of large dogs (especially the working breeds) are understandably concerned that their dogs might hurt smaller dogs. Here too socialization goes down hill and the big dog becomes increasingly snappy and scrappy. Now we're in vicious circle: the less the dog is socialized, the more likely he is to fight and thus be less socialized.

If your dog gets into a fight or is trying to protect herself from another dog, it actually sounds a LOT worse than it is. Yes there will be barking, growling and yelping going on, but 99.99% of the time it will be over even before you have had time to think.
Firstly and I know it's hard to do but don't panic!
DO NOT smother your pup/dog with hugs and kisses, this is the worst thing you can do because your dog will be in shock. Try not to pick her up or touch her, do not talk to her. The best thing to do is to walk her around in a circle (do not move too far away from the other dog, but make sure she is safe) after several minutes check her over for wounds, this is were your handling and inspection training comes in handy. 99% of the time there maybe no or little damage to either dogs if both dogs have good bite inhibition.

The Secret to Adolescent Success

Always make a point of praising your dog and offering a couple of treats whenever he eliminates in the right place. Keep a treat container by your dog's toilet area. You need to be there anyway to inspect and pick up your dog's faeces (before the stool becomes home and dinner for several hundred baby flies). Remember, you want your dog to want to eliminate in his toilet area and to be highly motivated to do so, even when he develops geriatric incontinence. Similarly, a stuffed Kong a day will continue to keep the behaviour doctor away. Your dog still needs some form of occupational therapy to idle away the time when left at home alone. Nothing will prevent household problems, such as destructive chewing, excessive barking, and hyperactivity, or alleviate boredom, stress, and anxiety as effectively as stuffing your dog's daily diet of kibble into a few Kongs. For your adolescent dog to continue to be reliably obedient and willingly compliant, you must integrate short training interludes, especially emergency sits and long settle-downs, into walks, play sessions, and your dog's other enjoyable day to-day activities. Maintaining your dog's manners through adolescence is easy if you know how to, but extremely difficult if you don't.

Should socialization ever fail and your dog snap, lunge, or nip, you will be thankful that you had the good sense to take your puppy to classes where he learned reliable bite inhibition. Your dog's defensive actions cause no harm but they warn you that you'd better quickly revamp your dog's socialization program and maintain his bite inhibition exercises before it happens again, which it will. Continue bite inhibition exercises indefinitely. Occasionally hand feed your dog and examine his muzzle and teeth (and maybe clean them) on a regular basis.

The secret to a well-socialized adult dog is at least one walk a day. Try to find different walks and different dog parks, so that your dog meets a variety of different dogs and people.
Socialization means training your dog to meet and get along with unfamiliar dogs and people. The only way to accomplish this is for your dog to continue meeting unfamiliar people and dogs daily. Praise your dog and offer a piece of kibble or high value treat every time he meets an unfamiliar dog or person.
And don't forget to maintain your own improved social life by inviting your friends over at least once a week, just to keep them still involved in training your dog. Ask them to bring along somebody new to meet your dog.
Host a puppy party and invite your dog's buddies from puppy class and the dog park. To offset some of the scarier aspects of the dog world at large—adult dogs, big dogs, and occasionally unfriendly dogs—make sure your adolescent dog has regular opportunity to socialize and play with his core companions.

Focus – Attention

If you want to train your puppy you are going to need to have her attention.
To start this exercise have your dog sitting in front of you, have a treat in your hand and hold your arm out to the side as far as you can, your pup will look at the treat for a long time, don't say anything to your pup. As soon as your pup makes eye contact and it will be very quick at first, treat and reward.
If your pup moves towards the treat hand, just simply start again and put your pup exactly where she was.
The reason we hold our hand out to the side is because we are looking for a definite head movement from your hand to your face. Continue to do this and try and do this as much as possible. If you have your dogs' full attention you will find it easier to train other command and you will find it easier to train with distractions.
Eventually the aim is to have your dog looking at you more than she's looking at the treat. When you have got to this stage, ask your

dog for a little bit longer. To start with your dog will look at you briefly as she's done before thinking why am I not getting this treat but if you just wait she will look at you longer.

When she looks at you for 2-3 seconds then you can introduce the cue I use 'watch me' but you can use 'watch' or 'look' etc.

The next stage will be to ask for a 'watch' command while you are walking together. This comes in handy later on in life as we don't know if your pup becomes anxious about bikes or joggers. So if you see a jogger approaching simply ask for the 'watch' getting your pups attention on you and only you, when the jogger has passed treat and praise your pup.

Toy play
Playing with your dog is really really important. It builds a better bond between puppy and owner. Let your puppy have only 3 toys at a time change them every couple of days and put the rest away, where your pup can't find them. Have one special toy that you and pup play with together. This will help with other commands such as

hold, give, and take it. If this toy is like a rope toy or a piece of suede with handles either end, you can play tug of war. This game is ok to play if you start and you finish the game. You can ask your pup to 'hold it' and 'give it', this is also a great impulse control game because once you have the toy in your hands your pup shouldn't take hold of the toy until you say so.
No matter what game you play with your pup, you start the game and you finish the game.

Sit

Each time the puppy approaches, have him sit. Slowly move a piece of kibble upwards, from in front of his nose to between his eyes. As the puppy raises his nose to sniff the kibble, he will lower his rear end and sit. If the puppy jumps up, you are holding the food lure too high. Repeat the procedure at this point do NOT say anything, puppies don't know what 'sit' means so get your puppy to do several repletion's (between 5 and 10) each time the puppy sits reward with a treat (kibble), once the puppy sits with out you having to lure too much then add the cue 'SIT'. Do this several times as dogs learn through repetition. (between 5 and 10) we need to do at least 5 repetitions so the dogs start to learn what we are asking her to do, but no more than 10 repetitions as the pup will only get bored, and we don't want that.

Sit to Say Hello (Meet and Greet)
As early as possible, establish sitting as the status quo for greeting people. Make sure each family member, visitor, or stranger has the puppy sit before they say hello, praise, pet, or offer a food reward. In no time, your puppy will learn to sit automatically when people approach. Sitting for praise or a food reward when greeting people certainly beats jumping up. And from the dog's viewpoint, sitting for attention, affection, and treats certainly beats getting punished for jumping up!

Down
Now have the puppy come, sit, and lie down. The pup should be in a sit this makes the down a lot easier for your puppy. Once the pup sits, lower a piece of kibble from just in front of his nose to between his front paws. Keep the puppy's nose on the treat as you move you hand to the floor, if the puppy's nose comes off your hand you've gone too quickly, your hand needs to move slowly, very slowly. As the puppy lowers his head to follow the food, he will usually lie down. If you try this on a slippery floor such as tiles or wooden floors the puppy's bottom slides down.

If your puppy stays in a sit with his head down just very slowly slide your hand underneath the puppy and he should go down.
If your puppy stands up every time the head goes down you will have to revert to plan B.
Plan B – sit on the floor with your legs out in front of you, bring your knees up. Try to lure your pup under your legs. You may have to start with your knees quite high to start with if your pup is a little bit timid. Lure your pup through once your pup is under your legs and in the down position, reward with a treat. Do this several times as dogs learn through repetition. (between 5 and 10) we need to do at least 5 repetitions so the dogs start to learn what we are asking her to do, but no more than 10 repetitions as the pup will only get bored, and we don't want that. Once the pup goes into the down position that's when you can add the cue 'DOWN'. So as the dog goes into position this is when you add the cue, eventually you want to be able to say 'DOWN' and the pup does it straight away.

Down from a stand
Once you pup knows the command 'Down', try teaching your pup a down from a stand rather than from a sit. We always start from a sit, but now we need to teach it from the stand this is the start of the **emergency down**. Have your pup in a standing position with a treat in your hand let the pup know you have a treat by putting it up to his nose and lure him down to the ground. Some pups will go into a bow position but if you wait the bottom will drop and you can

reward your pup with the treat and also saying 'down' to your dog. Hold on to the treat until your dog's bottom hits the floor, when it does treat him. Repeat this stage until you can stand by your dog say down and he cantilevers into the down position without going into a sit first.

Slowly increase the distance you are away from your pup, this is really difficult and it will take time to build up the distance. Eventually you can put your dog in a sit and wait walk away from your pup about 4ft away. Turn and face your pup and say down if you need to use a hand signal then do so, your puppy will read your body language. This is what's known as **Distance commands**.

Emergency down

For the **emergency down** ask your pup to sit and wait then walk away from your pup to about 10ft away call your pup (but in a different manner than if you want your pup to come to you as you are going to stop your pup before he gets to you) if you need Sarah to go through this with you just ask. So call your pup (use different Body language) when your pup is half way between where your pup was and you cue the pup 'Down' and he should go down.

If after you have given the down command your pup keeps coming try to meet him in the middle once your pup is in the down position, walk backwards to where you were standing, pause then return to your pup (who should still be in the down) and praise him but holding a treat near the floor, if you reward your pup quite high up you will be encouraging him to get up.

Once you have a reliable emergency down this way try doing it the other way when you pup is running away from you as apposed to coming towards you.

To do this, have your dog in a sit on your left hand side command wait and throw a toy or ball. Send you pup to fetch the toy then before he gets there command the down. If the pup goes down reward and praise, then ask him to go fetch the ball. So not only did he get praise and a treat from you the second part of the reward is going out to get the ball. When you have this your dog will be ready, in case of an emergency. Yes it's going to take time and patience but it's worth it. As I normally tell people the story about my own dog and how glad I am for putting in the training with him. As we were running along a track (The Ridgeway in Compton) he was running close to me as he normally does. There was a car coming he was only doing about 20 mph, but as the car approached my dog Sam suddenly wanted to cross the track? I shouted DOWN and he dropped into the down position about 3ft from the track where the car was. I believe it saved his life or certainly saved him from an injury. I believe this is an important command to teach.

Down and settle

When you sit down with your dog either on the floor or on the sofa (I'm not judging), say 'settle' when your dog is laying down quietly. They will soon associate the cue with what they are doing, this then means you can take your dog with you to cafes and pubs and they will settle under the table etc. this will also help with **table manners**. As you don't want your dog scrounging for scraps or even barking at you to give them food. Don't give into them.

Stand

This is probably the easiest of all the commands. Have your dog in a sit position and hold a treat about 6-8 inches away from you puppy's nose and if your hand is at the correct height your puppy will stand up on all 4's. If your hand is too high your puppy will come over and sit again, if your hand is too lower your puppy will come over and probably go into the down position. So it's important to keep your hand at nose level. I like to teach puppies the stand command as some dogs will need to go to the groomers and all dogs will go to the vet. So if pup knows the stand command it makes life easier.

Leave – NO need to say anything to your pup, let your pup work this out on his own.

Week one

In Hand - To start the leave command, have a treat in your hand and clench your hand into a fist. Hold your hand out to your pup (fingers/palm side up) let your pup lick, paw and nibble your hand as soon as your pup stops and moves away (the first time is going to be the longest and may take a while) do NOT talk to your puppy she needs to work it out for herself. Timing is crucial, you need to be quick. So as soon as puppy backs off and stops licking etc open your hand and give them the treat. Repeat several times, eventually what you want is to put your hand down to the dog and she leaves your hand. When she backs off straight away say 'LEAVE' then pause for a second or two then give her the treat. Then you can move to the next level.

On The Floor - Start with kneeling on the floor, have a treat in your hand and place treat hand, palm face down. As before let puppy lick, paw and sniff your hand, as soon as the puppy backs away PICK UP the treat and give it to your pup. ALWAYS pick up the treat and give it to your pup NEVER let the pup eat it off the floor. We are training our puppy to leave, so when we say leave the puppy must leave it not matter what. If you dropped something hot out of the oven or you dropped a tablet, you are not then going to say, yes take it.

Impulse control
Week three

In Hand - You have now got to the last level of this exercise, well done. So you can now hold a treat in your hand while your dog looks at it. This time when holding your hand out still I want you to just wait, don't say anything, but we are waiting for your pup to look at you (making eye contact) as soon as your pup looks at you, give her the treat. Again timing is critical.

On The Floor – Next step in to drop the treat from about 2 inches to start with, again if puppy moves towards it simply put your hand over the treat. If your pup watches the treat fall to the ground but remains still and leaving it, praise and reward with the treat. Continue to do this exercise at different heights don't push your puppy on to quickly (don't expect too much). Ideally we want to be able to drop something command the puppy 'leave' and then wait for the puppy to look at us, for the next instruction. It will happen, just be patient.

Recall

Many owners let their dogs off-lead without so much as a "please" or a "Sit." Often the dogs are excitedly bouncing and barking in anticipation of playing. Thus being let off-lead reinforces their boisterous behaviour. They delight in their newfound freedom, running around, sniffing, chasing each other, and playing together like crazy.

The owners look on and chat. Eventually, it's time to go. One owner calls her dog, the dog comes running, the owner snaps on the lead and the play session is over.

This sequence of events is likely to happen just once or twice, because on subsequent trips to the park the dog understandably will not be quite so keen to come to his owner when called. It doesn't take much for the dog to make the association between coming when called and having an otherwise utterly enjoyable run in the park abruptly terminated. On future trips to the park, the dog approaches his owner slowly with head down. The owner is now doing a fine job de-motivating the dog's recall and is inadvertently training the dog **not** to come when called.

Indeed, slow recalls quickly become no recalls, as the dog tries to prolong his fun by playing Catch-Me-If-You-Can. The irritated owner now screams for the dog to come, "Bad dog! Come here!" And, of course, the dog muses, "I don't think so! In the past I have learned that nasty tone and volume mean you're not too happy. I think it would foolish for me to approach you right now. You're not in the best frame of mind to praise and reward me appropriately." But you are not going to do this with your dog, are you?

Your puppy should not be off lead until you have a 100% recall. The recall is one of the most important commands you will teach your dog, it could **save your dog life**.

Start in the house call your dog's name followed by the cue 'Come'. Make this a game as puppy comes to you run backwards until puppy actually gets to you. Praise and reward like mad.

Next move to the garden using a long training line (not a retractable lead) call your puppy while she's walking around use her name to get her attention then 'Come' only say this command once as you don't want to dilute the command by repeating it and not getting any results.

So dogs name, and then 'come'. If your puppy doesn't come give a little tug on the line (this is saying to the puppy 'hey, I'm talking to you), if puppy still isn't coming then reel her in gently using the training line. Praise and reward by touching but NO treats as you have had to do the work for her.

Let your puppy wander around again (you may need to walk away from puppy) repeat the exercise as above. Dogs name and then 'come' if puppy comes first time then praise, lots of fuss and a high value treats (cocktail sausage, cheese, chicken). Repeat this several times (between 5 and 10 reps). You will find your puppy comes every time. When your puppy does something for the first time, like coming to you for the first time, or the first time she comes to you while distracted rather than giving her one treat break that treat into about 5 pieces your puppy will think she's done a brilliant job and is likely going to do it again.

Next stage is to find a quiet corner in a play field and repeat the above. Once you have a reliable recall in a quiet space start working on some distractions maybe a dog across the field, a cyclist or a jogger. Working at a distance first then getting closer and closer.

You could let your dogs sniff and say hello to other dogs and call them away from this distraction. Send your puppy off on her way again you could say 'ok' or 'go sniff'.

The collar grab
If your pup was to run out of the front door unexpectedly you need to be able to take the dog by the collar without him backing off every time you reach out for her collar. With the puppy on lead and wearing a collar (not a harness). Hold the handle of the lead in your right hand with a treat between your forefinger and thumb. With your left hand starting at the handle of the lead run your left hand down the lead towards the puppy's collar, when your hand reaches the collar grab hold of the collar and reward by giving the treat from your right hand, repeat this several times. This lets your puppy know that grabbing the collar is a good thing and not to be nervous of. You can also use this in a similar way while out walking off lead. We need the puppy to understand that grabbing the collar doesn't mean its end of the play session or we're going home now. Call your puppy when your puppy reaches you grab the collar and give him a treat then release the collar and say 'go play' or 'go sniff' this should be done a couple of times on each walk. If commands are not reinforced your puppy will forget the commands, so keep it all going.

Collar Grab
Twenty percent of dog bites occur when a family member reaches to grab the dog by the scruff or collar. One doesn't need to be a

rocket scientist to figure this out. Obviously, the dog has learned that when people grab the collar bad things often happen. Consequently, the pup becomes hand-shy, plays Catch Me-if-You-Can, or reacts defensively.

It is potentially dangerous to have a pup dodge you when you reach for his collar. For example, you need to know you could effectively grab your dog if he ever tried to dash out the front door. So teach your puppy to enjoy being grabbed by the collar. First, prevent your pup from forming negative associations to human hands, and second, teach your pup that being taken by the collar has only positive consequences.

1. If you let your puppy play without interruption, and then take him by the collar to end the play session, of course he will come to dislike you reaching for his collar because a collar grab signals the end of the play session. Starting in the house and later in the park, frequently interrupt puppy play sessions by taking your puppy by the collar, asking him to sit, praising him, offering a piece of kibble, and then letting him go play again. The puppy thus learns that being taken by the collar is not necessarily the end of the play session. Instead, a collar grab is a short timeout for refreshment and a few kind words from his owner before the puppy gets to play again. Also, every time you interrupt the play session, you may use resumption of play to reward your puppy for sitting and allowing you to take him by the collar.

2. If you lead or drag your puppy into confinement, he will no doubt come to dislike being taken by the collar, and he will dislike confinement. Instead, teach your puppy to enjoy confinement. Stuff a bunch of hollow chew toys with kibble, put them in your puppy's confinement area, and then close the door with your puppy on the outside. In no time at all, your puppy will beg to go inside. Now simply instruct your pup, "Go to your bed (or crate)" or "Go to your playroom (long-term confinement area)," and open the door. Your

pup will happily rush inside and settle down peacefully with his chew toys.

3. Above all, promise your puppy that you will never (never) call your puppy and then grab him by the collar to reprimand or punish. Doing this just once will make him hate coming when called and hate when you reach for his collar. If you punish your puppy after he comes to you, he will take longer to come the next time. Eventually slow recalls will become no recalls. Your puppy will still misbehave; only now you will be unable to catch him! If you ever punish your puppy after taking his collar, he will soon become hand-shy, evasive, and defensive.

So, let's teach your pup to accept that the grabbing of the collar is a good thing. Have your dog on lead, hold the lead and have a treat in the lead hand, run the other hand down the lead (slowly at first) put your hand in the collar and reward whilst still holding the collar. Remember repetition, so if this behaviour has become a problem I would suggest doing this exercise daily and several times a day and especially out on walks.

Wait
Wait and stay are 2 separate exercises. Wait means wait there because I'm going to ask you to do something else (such as a recall)
To start the wait exercise, put your pup in a sit. Using a flat hand (palm facing your pup) as a hand signal say the cue 'wait' take one step away then return to your pup, if your pup is still sitting reward and gently praise (don't over do it with the praise because we are asking the pup to wait and to stay calm). If your pup comes with you when you step away try, putting your dog in a sit use the flat hand to command the wait say the cue 'wait' but do not move stay as still as possible. Wait for a second then reward and praise. Do this several times before you try stepping away. Build up on the distance and the duration. Start in the house, then the garden and then out on walks. If the puppy gets up it's because you have either gone too far or you have left her too long. Set her up to succeed.

Stay
Stay means stay there because I'm coming back to you
Start with your dog on your left hand side in a sit position, command 'stay' and use a flat hand command while giving the verbal cue. This also shows the puppy you have not treats in your hand (if you did your puppy would follow you and not stay). So once you have commanded the 'stay' take one step to your right and then back to the left, so you are back to your puppy's side if your puppy is still in the sit position reward with a treat and gentle praise. Don't get your puppy too excited at this point. Repeat up to 5-10 times. Slowly increase the distance and then slowly increase duration the puppy is left. If your puppy gets up then you have either gone too far away or you have left your puppy too long. Set your puppy up to succeed every time.

Food Manners
Now your puppy knows 'sit' and 'wait' use it in many different situations, such as sit and wait at doorways, sit and wait while you unlock the boot of your car etc.
'Sit' and 'wait' while I get your food ready. Put your dog in a sit and wait, slowly lower the dogs' food down to the floor if your puppy gets up, take the food bowl up and start again. This might

take some time but if you persist you will have your pup sitting and waiting when the bowl is on the floor you can cue your puppy to eat his food. **Impulse control** - When your pup is sitting and waiting patiently for his dinner, if he's looking at his food on the floor, just wait him out; wait until he looks at you. Then say to him 'good boy, ok'.

Car manners.

Command wait and slowly open the car door. if Pup moves close the door slightly making sure you don't shut pup's paw in the door. Never let you pup just jump out of the car suddenly. you could even set up the situation and have the car door open, put puppy on the car seat and just ask for a wait after a short pause mark that behaviour with 'Yes good boy' and treat. This can be done on the back seat or in the boot of your car. If you have a crate to keep puppy safe, make sure puppy is calm while you open the crate door, never open when your pup is really excited, your pup should wait until you are ready for him to come out.

Examination of your pup

Your puppy needs to let you, your vet and possible the groomer to touch him all over, so every now and then just check and rub your dog when grooming him. Every couple of days just check his eyes are clean, his ears are clean (if his ears are dirty clean them with a moist cotton wool pad, if they are dirty again a few days later it maybe quite serious like an ear infection which needs vet treatment. Check his paws as there maybe a grass seed, or there maybe a cut on his pad. Check your puppy has no fleas or ticks (these can be life threatening) and make sure your pup has no lumps and bumps. If you are concerned about anything it is worth letting your vet have a look. If its left it will only get worst, not only will you puppy suffer it will cost you more in vets' bills.

Hold and Give

Teach your puppy hold and give can be useful, especially if your dog picks something up he shouldn't have like a pair of socks.
To teach the 'hold' put a ball on the floor and try and get your pup interested in it by rolling it from side to side, as soon as your pup puts his mouth on it say 'hold' and praise him. If this is done often enough have your pup in a sit and place a ball in front of him and say 'Hold' while pointing and looking at the ball. Once your pup knows hold you can then move to the 'Give'.
Have your pup sitting in front of you and ask him to hold the ball, (don't let go of the ball) once he has hold of the ball take the ball from your pup when he releases the ball say 'give' and praise. If your pup has a habit of running off with the ball either use a training line or hold the collar to stop him running away, once he realizes its more fun getting your attention by praising and treating, than when you ignore him running off with it. Eventually your pup will know the word 'Give' and will give you everything he might have in his mouth.
If your pup loves to run off with (check page 11 on how to teach leave) socks etc, use that item and work with it. Place it in front of your dog ask the dog to hold it, give it and even leave it. Don't ask your dog to hold an item if you have told him to leave it, as leave it means leave it and he shouldn't touch it at all. So don't give him mixed messages.

The Dog Walk

As soon as it is safe for your puppy to go out, take him on walks. Bear in mind you don't want to over exercise your puppy 5 minutes per month. There is no better overall socialization exercise and no better overall training exercise. As an added benefit, dog walks are good for your health, heart, and soul. Walk that dog! Doggy socialization is good for your social life too

To start with your puppy will scratch at the collar this is normal until they get use to it. Leave the collar on 24/7, if you take it off while the puppy is in the house it's going to take her longer to get use to it and you may need it for unwanted behaviours like jumping up.
So once you have the collar on, call your puppy to you ask for a sit and pop the lead on, if your puppy gets up while you are putting the lead on just stop and ask for the sit and start again. Be patient with your puppy don't rush any training with your puppy.
Start by walking your dog on lead around the house and the garden. Many puppies but the brakes on and sit or pull backwards this is normal, DON'T use the lead to pull your puppy to you but use your voice, body language and treats to encourage your puppy to walk.

Teaching Loose Lead Walking
There are 2 ways of teaching your puppy loose lead walking.
  1. **Flat hand with treat.**

Choose a side which you prefer to have your puppy to walk on. I work my dogs on my left. So if you choose to have your puppy on your left hand side have the lead handle in your right hand so the lead crosses your body. Once you have your pup on your left and the lead in your right hand, this leaves your left hand free for treats.

Hold your left hand flat with your palm upwards place a piece of food to the left hand side of your palm and place your thumb on top. Now place your hand down palm facing towards your dogs' nose and then walk with your puppy sniffing and nibbling away at the treat, every 5 paces treat and say your cue 'heel' or 'close'. Then after every 10 paces and increase the number of paces gradually. This shows your pup where she needs to be when on the lead.

2. **C shape training.**

You can also show your pup where 'Heel' or 'Close' is. Have your pup sitting in front of you (no need to be on lead) have a treat in your left hand lure your pup out in a big 'C' shape, so go out to your left hand side around behind you straighten your pup up and lure her into the heel work position, this is where you say your command either 'Heel' or 'Close' (if you need Sarah to demonstrate this please ask. This is called a German finish in the world of competition obedience. This is also how assistant pups are trained. It's really that effective. You just need to be consistent and patient. If you, family members and dog walkers use this method your pup will know where she needs to be. You will not have a dog that pulls on lead later on in life; you won't need to buy different collars, harnesses and leads etc if you put the effort in now. Never let your pup walk in front of you.

Don't use a harness to walk your dog these only allow your pup to put his whole body weight into it and you have no control – use a flat collar or a half check collar for larger dogs.
Always take treats or kibble out on walks, when people/children/joggers/cyclists pass you and your dog reward her for not reacting. If you can see a little anxiety in your dog make sure the leads is loose, but still maintain the lead in a short manner just in case she lunges. Also make sure you are relaxed and calm – very important.
Praise and reward your dog for greeting unfamiliar dogs and people.

If you have a large rescue dog you may need a head collar, Halti head collars are badly designed so I would highly recommend a Dogmatic head collar.

Here are a few dos and don'ts for teaching your dog to walk calmly on-lead:

DO practice lead walking around your house and garden from the very beginning and take your puppy for walks in public as soon as he is old enough.

DON'T wait until your dog reaches adolescence before trying to teach him to walk on-lead in public, unless you wish to provide amusement for onlookers.

DO alternate short periods of 15 to 30 seconds, when your dog walks by your side, with longer periods of a minute or so, when your dog is allowed to range and sniff at the end of the lead. This motivates your dog to walk by your side, as walking side-by-side is regularly reinforced by permission to range and sniff.

DON'T expect your adolescent (or adult) dog to endlessly heel. He will learn that heeling is mutually exclusive to ranging and sniffing. He won't want to heel and will grow to resent training and the trainer (you) for spoiling his fun.

DON'T allow your dog to decide when to pull on lead. Employ red light/green light training. When your dog tightens the lead, immediately stop, stand still, and wait. By now your dog will know what 'heel' means and should come to your side, if your dog becomes stubborn and resides not to do as you say then guide her back (in a C shape) back to your side. You may need to have to go back to basics with an adolescent dog, but don't worry if you continue with what you were taught in puppy class and this booklet you can't go wrong.

Don't let your puppy pull you to a side he wants to sniff. If you do he will learn he can pull you, whenever he wants to sniff. You decide where to let your puppy sniff or not. So while out your puppy should either be a heel or go sniff.

Doggy Door Manners

1. The walk needs to start off in a calm manner. Starting with the lead (harness), when the lead comes out your dog need to stay calm. Set your dog up in a sit, calmly put on the lead if the dog moves stop, stay calm and start again. Your dog needs to know he will go out quicker if she stays calm.
2. Once the lead is on move to the front door put your pup in a sit and wait. Proceed to open the door if your pup gets up shut the door, continue to do this until your pup is sitting with the door open, gentle praise as we don't want her to get up.
3. With your dog in a sit, command 'wait', if need be walk backwards out the door, once out call your pup through and praise. If you are backing out of the door and your dog moves towards you, don't worry just go back and start again. Remember calm, patient and consistency will get you everything. Call her through the door when you are ready.
4. Once your pup and you are out the front door command a sit while you lock up etc and reward her.

All of the above can be done in separate training steps, so if you have problems with point 3 but 1, 2 and 4 are brilliant make a point of just training point number 3.

Now you are ready for the walk, continue to as you were in puppy training, either hold a treat under your thumb with a flat hand or if your dog pulls, you need to stop and guide your dog round in a big 'C' shape back to your side. Be consistent it will happen and you will enjoy your walks more. Because in adolescence, dog's will push the owners to see what she can get away with you need to keep up with ALL your training, if one person in the house doesn't reinforce the commands and lets the dog jump up for cuddles I'm afraid you are fighting a loosing battle. EVERYONE who is around the dog whether its owners, dog walker, pet sitters etc. its up to you as a dog owner to make sure everyone is reading from the same book.

WARNING: Don't over exercise your puppy golden rule of thumb is 5 minutes per month (old) so if you puppy is 4 months old then no more than 20 minutes per day. This can be broken down into 2 separate walks of 10 minutes if you like, but no more than this. If you have a really hyper puppy and you think she needs more exercise, she doesn't if anything play more mental stimulation games this will calm her down. Over exercising your puppy can also increase their excitement and hype them up even more. Yes dogs have their 5 minutes of zoomies once or twice a day but this is fine, let them burn off any excess energy. The reason we don't exercise too much is because a puppy's bones are still very soft and the bones have growth plates if either of these are damaged your puppy may suffer later in life. Also don't let a young puppy (up to the age of 12 months) JUMP.

So this includes jumping off sofas, running up and down the stairs, jumping out of cars etc. If you have fairly large dogs try and take some of the weight from the dog so the impact isn't great. If you want to do agility with your dog, clubs won't let you start until the pup is over 12 months because of this reason. If you want to start agility with your pup you can get your dog to walk over poles rather than jumping over them, you can teach the weave poles and going through tunnels etc but NO jumping.

If you train your pup on every walk, you will soon have a puppy that will sit quickly and settle down promptly with a single request, no matter how excited or distracted he may be. Moreover, your dog settles down willingly and happily because he knows that being told to lie down is not the end of the world and not even the end of the walk. Your dog will have learnt that "Settle Down," for example, is just a relaxing time-out with gentle praise before his exciting life as Walking Dog resumes. With your now-mannerly pup, you'll find that it is quicker navigating country roads and suburban pathways than with your previously hyperactive hound. Now you can follow your intended itinerary without being pulled every which way but loose.

Tablet taking

From time to time your puppy will need to take tablets. So every now and then when you have some treats on you, just open your dog's mouth as if you were giving her a tablet. Pop in a treat, this shows your pup that when you open her month in this way doesn't necessarily mean a bad horrible taste is coming. When you do need to give your dog a tablet pop in a couple of treats in with the tablet, so it's not too bad for her.

Toilet training

The more quickly you house training your puppy, the sooner she will get to enjoy free run of your house.

Whenever you are away from home, leave your puppy in her playroom/utility room or crate. A suitable long-term confinement area needs a waterproof (easy-to clean) floor, a comfortable bed, a bowl of fresh water, some chew toys stuffed with kibble, and a puppy pad.

Housetraining Is as Easy as 1-2-3
When you are away from home, keep your puppy confined to her puppy playroom, where she has a suitable doggy toilet (puppy pad). Otherwise, when you are at home: 1. Keep your puppy closely confined to her doggy den.
2. Every hour on the hour, release your pup from confinement and quickly run her (on-lead if necessary) to the toilet area. To start with when you see your puppy go wee use your cue command, 'wee-wees' for example then treat her when she's finished same as with the number 2's. It's best to walk very slowly around the garden without talking to your puppy. Your puppy will not be able to concentrate on what she's meant to be doing if you talk to her.
3. Enthusiastically praise your puppy, offer her three freeze-dried liver treats, and then play/train indoors. (Once your puppy is full vaccinated, take her for a walk as a reward for eliminating in her toilet area.)

Common Mistakes
1. Allowing your puppy to make a mistake. And why did the pup make a mistake? Let's ask her teacher. Who left the puppy with a full rectum and full bladder unattended in the bedroom? Who left the empty puppy unattended to ransack the living room? Who allowed the untrained puppy to be home alone with free run of the house?

2. Not rewarding your puppy for getting it right. You didn't praise your pup or offer any tasty treats, and now you wonder why your puppy doesn't do what you want her to do. It is hardly your puppy's fault that she feels free to improvise her doggy toys and toilets.
3. NEVER shout at your puppy or pick them up and put them outside. If you do, in the puppies eyes they have just been shouted at for no reason, then they get put outside

Use Stain and odour sprays as this will stop the puppy repeating any accidents.
DO NOT shout or tell your puppy off, this WILL make toilet training harder the best thing to do if you see a puddle of wee or a stool is to remove the puppy from the room calmly, don't say anything to the puppy. Clean up the mess and spray with stain and

odour, then let your puppy back in the room without looking or specking to your puppy.

By doing this you are not showing the puppy your frustration, the slightest hint of frustration will be passed to the puppy and will upset your pup, which then means the pup will continue to soil in the house.

Jumping up

If your puppy jumps up to greet you or family and friends you need to nip this in the bud quickly. When out walking you will find you don't get far until you meet someone who wants to say hello and fuss your dog. Your puppy will naturally want to jump up to say hello.

As a responsible dog owner you will need to be firm with these people as they will say things such as 'oh, it doesn't matter' or 'I don't mind'.

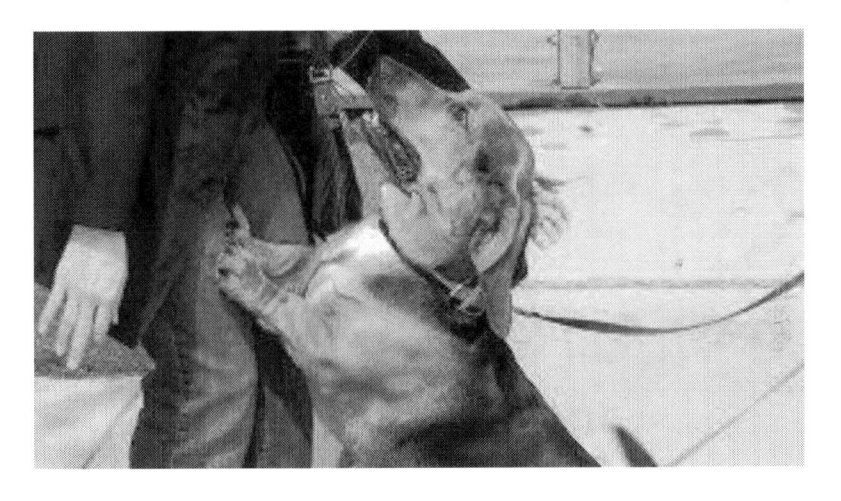

To stop your dog jumping up when you come in from work or when you see your puppy first thing in the morning put your finger in the collar and hold her down so all four feet are on the ground, then you can give her a fuss.

This should apply to visitors who may come to visit you and people out on walks.

If your puppy has already jumped up on you put your finger in the collar and say 'OFF' in a firm but friendly voice.

When dogs are naughty, say they may be barking, jumping up etc you don't want to talk, look or touch them. This is giving them your attention and we don't want to give them our attention at this time, they can however have our attention when they are behaving nicely. Your puppy only wants to please you.

So if your dog is barking don't join in by shouting at your dog. Don't stroke your dog while she's barking, don't push your dog down when she jumps up etc.

Home Alone

All owners find it occasionally necessary to leave their puppy dog at home alone. So before leaving your puppy for long periods, you should teach him how to amuse himself appropriately when left alone, such as by chewing stuffed chew toys, and learning how to enjoy his own company without becoming anxious or stressed. A pup is a highly social animal and therefore requires adequate preparation for spending some of his time in social isolation.

To teach your puppy how to settle down calmly and quietly when you are absent, start by teaching him to settle down with a chew toy at times when you are present.

You must teach him to settle down and shush. Right from the outset, make frequent quiet moments part of the puppy's daily routine. Additionally, encourage your puppy to settle down beside you for longer and longer periods. For example, when you're watching television have your pup lie down on lead or in his crate, but release him for short play-training breaks during the commercials.
For a young puppy, you can't have too many rules. When playing with your pup, have him settle down for frequent short interludes every one or two minutes. Initially have the pup lie still for a few seconds before letting him play again. After a minute, interrupt the play session once more with a three-second settle-down.
Then try for four seconds, then five, eight, ten, and so on. Although being yo-yoed between the commands "Settle down" and "Let's play" is difficult at first, the puppy soon learns to settle down quickly and happily. Your puppy will learn that being asked to settle down is not the end of the world, nor is it necessarily the end of the play session, but instead that "Settle down" signals a short timeout and reward break before he is allowed to resume playing.

If you teach your puppy to be calm and controlled when told, you will have years of fun and excitement ahead. Once your puppy has learnt to settle down and shush on cue, there is so much more your dog can enjoy with you. Your well-trained dog is likely to be invited for many walks, trips in the car, picnics, and visits to the pub, or to Grandma's, and even on incredible journeys to stay in ritzy dog-friendly hotels.

If your pup has not been taught to settle down by the time he reaches adolescence, he will be unfit to be taken places. Your pup will begin a lifetime of confinement and isolation at home while the rest of the family go out to have a good time. Not fair!

Separation Anxiety

Maintaining your puppy's confinement schedule when you are at home prepares your puppy to be calm when you are gone. Allowing a young puppy unrestricted access to you when you are at home quickly encourages him to become overly dependent, and overdependence is the most common reason why dogs become anxious when left at home alone. Try your best to teach your puppy to enjoy his own company, to develop self-confidence, and to stand on his own four paws. Once your puppy is confident and relaxed on his own, he may enjoy all of his time with you when you are at home.

When leaving your puppy for hourly sessions in his short-term confinement area (dog crate), make a point to check how he fares when left in another room. For example, periodically confine your puppy to his crate in the dining room while you prepare food in the kitchen, then keep the pup in his crate in the kitchen while the family eats dinner in the dining room.

Most importantly, when you are at home, make certain to familiarize your puppy with his long-term confinement area (puppy playroom). Confining your pup when you're home enables you to monitor his behaviour during confinement and check in on him at irregular intervals, quietly rewarding him for being quiet. Thus your pup will not necessarily associate his confinement area with your absence, but rather he will learn to look forward to time spent in his playroom with his special toys. Give your puppy plenty of toys whenever leaving him on his own. Ideal chew toys are indestructible and hollow (such as Kong products), as they may be conveniently stuffed with kibble and occasional treats which periodically fall out and reward the pup for chewing his toy. If your puppy is gainfully occupied with his chew toy, he will fret less over your absence.

Additionally, leave a radio playing. The sound will provide white noise to mask outside disturbances. The sound of a radio is also reassuring, since it is normally associated with your presence.

When leaving your puppy the first 20 minutes is the worst, so gradually increase the time your puppy is left up to 20 minutes. If your puppy is quite happy to be left for 20 minutes she should be ok to be left for longer.

When Leaving Home
Make sure to stuff a number of chew toys with kibble and treats. Make sure to stuff a piece of freeze-dried liver into the tiny hole of each Kong, or deep into the marrow cavity of each bone. Place the tastily stuffed chew toys in your puppy's long-term confinement area and shut the door . . . with your puppy on the outside! When your puppy begs you to open the door, let him in and shut the door, turn on the radio or television, and leave quietly. Your puppy's chewing will be regularly reinforced by each piece of kibble which falls out of the chew toy. Your puppy will continue to chew in an attempt to extract the freeze-dried liver. Eventually your puppy will fall asleep. Chewing also relieves stress so if the puppy is slightly stressed as he's on his own the chew toys will help.

When Returning Home
Do not acknowledge your puppy's presence with praise or petting until he retrieves a chew toy. Once he brings you a chew toy, use a pen or pencil to push out the piece of freeze dried liver which your puppy has been unable to extract. This will impress your puppy to no end.

Jekyll-and-Hyde
Behaviour smothering your puppy with attention and affection when you are home primes the pup to really miss you when you are gone. A Jekyll-and-Hyde environment (lots of attention when you

are there, and none when you are gone) quickly creates a Jekyll and-Hyde puppy which is completely confident when you are there, but falls apart and panics when you are gone. If you allow your puppy to become dependent upon your presence, he will be anxious in your absence. Canine anxiety is bad news for you and bad news for your pup. When stressed, dogs are more likely to indulge in bad habits, such as house soiling, chewing, digging, and barking. Being anxious is also decidedly unpleasant for your pup. During your puppy's first few weeks at home, frequent confinement with stuffed chew toys is essential for your pup to develop confidence and independence. Once your puppy is quite happy busying himself with his chew toys whenever left alone, you may safely allow you're now well behaved and confident pup to enjoy as much time with you as he likes, without the fear that he will become anxious in your absence.

Crate Training

Short-term confinement to a crate has many advantages: it prevents your puppy from making mistakes around the house; maximizes the likelihood the pup will develop a chew toy habit; and facilitates housetraining because you may now accurately predict when your puppy needs to relieve herself. If your puppy chews her bed, remove it for a couple of days until the pup has become fixated on chew toys.

The purpose of short-term confinement is:
1. To prevent mistakes around the house
2. To teach your puppy to become a chew toyaholic (since chew toys stuffed with food are the only chewable available), so that she learns to settle down quickly, quietly, and calmly
3. To be able to predict when your puppy needs to eliminate closely confining a puppy to her bed strongly inhibits urination and defecation, so she will be in dire need to relieve herself when released from the crate each hour. Being able to accurately predict when your puppy needs to eliminate enables you to be there to teach her where to eliminate, and to reward the pup for doing the right thing in the right place at the right time.

Confidence

Your dog needs to be confident. The way to grow her confidence is to praise every good behaviour, show her what you want her to do, and then praise her for getting it right. Don't leave her to make her own choice and get it wrong. If she does make the wrong choices don't punish her as this will knock her confidence. Instead just show her what you want her to do. Its best to show your pup how to behave then praise, rather that let her get it wrong and tell her off or punish her. If you get in the habit of telling her off it will spiral out of control.

Socialization with People (by 3 months of age)

Raising and training a pup to be people-friendly is the second most important goal of pet-dog husbandry. Remember, teaching bite inhibition is always the most important goal. But during your pup's first month at home, urgency dictates that socialization with people is the prime puppy directive. Your puppy must be fully socialized to people before he is three months old. Many people think puppy classes are the time to socialize puppies to people. Not so. It's too little, and too late. Puppy classes are a fun night out to continue socializing socialized puppies with people, for therapeutic socialization of puppies with other puppies, and most important, for puppies to learn bite inhibition. You now have just a few weeks left to socialize your puppy. Unfortunately, your pup needs to be confined indoors until he is at least three months old, when he has acquired sufficient immunity through his puppy vaccinations against the more serious dog diseases. However, even a relatively short period of social isolation at such a crucial developmental stage could all but ruin your puppy's temperament. Whereas dog-dog socialization may be put on temporary hold until your pup is old enough to go to puppy classes and the dog park, you simply cannot delay socialization with people. It may be possible to live with a dog that does not like other dogs, but it is difficult and potentially dangerous to live with a dog that does not like people, especially if the dog doesn't like some of your friends and family. Consequently, there is considerable urgency to introduce your puppy to a wide variety of people—to family, friends, strangers, and especially men, and children. As a rule of thumb, your pup needs to meet at least a hundred different people before he is three months old—an average of three unfamiliar people a day.

Urgency
From the very first day you get your puppy, the clock is ticking. And time flies! By eight weeks of age, your puppy's Critical Period of Socialization is already waning and within a month, his most impressionable learning period will start to close. There is so much to teach, and nearly everything needs to be taught right away.

Warning
If your puppy is slow to approach, or doesn't approach your guests, do something about it now. Certainly your puppy may be shy, but he is also frighteningly under socialized. It is absolutely abnormal for a two- to three-month-old puppy not to eagerly approach people. You must resolve this problem within one week. Otherwise, it will rapidly get worse—much worse. If you let the days slip by, future attempts at therapeutic socialization will become progressively less

effective. Please do not ignore your puppy's fears by rationalizing: "He takes a while to warm to strangers." If your pup takes a while to warm to strangers now, he will likely be intolerant and scared of strangers as an adult. It is simply not fair to let your puppy grow up to be scared and anxious around people. Please help your puppy today.

The solution is simple and effective, and usually only takes one week. For the next seven days, invite over half a dozen different people each day to handfeed your puppy's meals. For just one week, your puppy must not receive any food from family members or in his dog bowl. This technique works quickly if your puppy only receives kibble and treats from the hands of household guests. Once the puppy happily accepts food from the hand, your guests may then ask the pup to come, sit, and lie down for each piece of kibble. Your guests will soon become your puppy's new best friends.

Hand feeding

1. Hand feeding teaches your puppy to like kibble. Kibble may then be used effectively as lures and rewards for handling and gentle exercises and for basic training, especially by children, men, and strangers.
2. Hand feeding teaches your puppy to like training and his trainers, especially children, men, and strangers.
3. Teaching your puppy "Off" and "Take it" will help prevent her from becoming a food guarder.
4. Teaching your puppy "Take it . . . Gently" is the very core of your puppy's developing a soft mouth and learning bite inhibition. Hand feeding enables you to choose convenient times for teaching your pup to control his jaws, rather than having to deal with your puppy whenever he decides to play-bite and bother you. Hand feeding is very effective if your dog is boisterous, through adolescence, aggressive to humans and dogs.

A Very Important Rule
It is so easy (and quick) to change your pups personality. One single person can have a dramatic impact on your puppy's personality—for better or worse. Insist that nobody—nobody—interact or play with your puppy until they demonstrate they can get him to come eagerly, sit promptly, and lie down calmly. Untrained visitors, especially children and adult male friends and relatives, are renowned for ruining good puppies in short order. If your visitors won't listen and wise up, put your puppy in his long-term confinement area, or ask the visitors to leave.

Be Safe
Puppies may become infected with serious dog diseases by sniffing the urine or faeces of infected dogs. Never let your puppy on the ground where other dogs may have eliminated. You may take your puppy for car rides and to visit friends, but always carry your puppy from house to car, and vice versa. Of course, these precautions also apply to visits to the veterinary clinic. The ground immediately outside the door of the clinic and the floor of the waiting room are two of the most likely contaminated areas. Carry your puppy from the car to the clinic and keep him on your lap in the waiting room. Better yet, keep your puppy crated in your car until it is time for his examination.

Puppies and Children
For puppy owners with children, the next few months present a bit of a challenge. It is infinitely worthwhile, however, because puppies successfully socialized with children generally develop exceedingly sound temperaments—they have to—and once they mature there is little in life that can surprise or upset them. However, to maximize the relationship between dogs and children and to ensure the dog's good nature and solid disposition, parents must educate their children as well as the pup. Teach your children how to act around the pup, and teach your pup how to act around children.

Three Goals of Socialisation

1. Teach your puppy to enjoy the presence, actions, and antics of all people—first the family, and then friends and then strangers, especially children and men. Adult dogs tend to feel most uneasy around children and men, especially little boys. A dog's antipathy toward children and men is more likely to develop if the puppy grows up with few or none around, and if the puppy's social contacts with children and men have been unpleasant or scary.

2. Teach your puppy to enjoy being hugged and handled (restrained and examined) by people, especially by children, veterinarians, and groomers. Specifically, teach your puppy to enjoy being touched and handled in a variety of "hot spots," namely, around his collar, muzzle, ears, paws, tail, and rear end.

3. Teach your puppy to enjoy giving up valued objects when requested, especially her food bowl, bones, balls, chew toys, garbage, and paper tissues.

Training Treats

To prevent your puppy from porking out on junk food treats, use your pup's daily ration of kibble as training treats. To

prevent your puppy from being overfed by members of the family, measure your puppy's daily diet of kibble plus treats into a separate container first thing in the morning. Thus at any time of the day, if any kibble or treats remain in the container, they may be fed to the puppy as a snack, as a meal, or individually handfed as rewards when training.

Give every guest a bag of training treats so that your puppy will be inclined to like them from the outset. Show your guests how you use your puppy's dinner kibble to lure/reward train him to come, sit, lie down, and roll over. Ask your puppy to come. Praise him profusely as he approaches and give him a piece of kibble when he arrives. Back up and do it again. Repeat the sequence several times.

Men

Many adult dogs are more fearful of men than they are of women. So invite over as many men as possible to handle and gentle your puppy. It is especially important to invite men to socialize with your puppy if no men are living in the household.

Strangers Young puppies tend to be universally accepting and tolerant of all people, but, unless taught otherwise, adolescent and adult dogs predictably develop a natural wariness of people they do not know. Introducing your puppy to a hundred people before he is three months old will help make him more accepting of strangers as an adolescent. To remain continually accepting of strangers, however, your adult dog needs to continually meet strangers. Meeting the same people over and over just won't do it. Your adult dog needs to meet new people each day, so you must maintain your newly improved social life at home or walk your dog regularly.

Punishment

I find it best to teach your pup how to behave so you can praise and enjoy each others company rather than letting the dog do what she wants, which is unacceptable and then having to correct the dog.

Dog training has changed so much over the last 20-30 years, for the better. Positive reward training works so much quicker and easier for owner and pup/dog. Basically if your dog is misbehaving it's because you haven't taught her the correct way to behave, so don't tell her off or punish her. Because she know, no better.

If you tell your puppy off for chewing the furniture, barking at neighbours, and digging in the garden all you are doing is knocking her confidence. She will not trust you, she will not want to be with you, and she may run off.
If you effectively use reward-training techniques, punishment is seldom necessary.
In fact, when you use fun and games, reward based training methods, banishment is the all-time most effective punishment—a short timeout with no more training game, no more rewards, and no more you.
Simply ignoring your pup and not playing with your pup is enough punishment or treating one dog but not the other if you have 2 or more dogs.

Time outs!
Time outs are a good way of telling your dog that's not on. Time outs include the following and if done correctly work very efficiently.
The toilet – if your dog barks, bites, nips or has any other unwanted behaviour you can put your puppy in the downstairs toilet for 20 seconds. Make sure your puppy can't get to toilet rolls etc. Being away from the owner gives them time to think about what they have done and will associate the confinement with the behaviour and there for the behaviour decreases or stops altogether.

Another way to time out your pup is - when your pup is on the lead you can hold the lead in your right then hold your hand out to the side, make sure the puppy isn't touching your body. Don't talk, look or touch your puppy. Hold him there for about 20 seconds. Release the pressure and loosen the lead.

Handling/Examination

Teaching your eight-week-old puppy to enjoy being handled and examined is as easy as it is essential. Your pup's veterinarian, trainer, and groomer will be forever grateful, as will be you and your puppy. It is a truly unfortunate puppy that finds it scary to be handled and examined. Many dogs have a number of "hot spots," which if not defused in puppy hood can be extremely sensitive to touch. Handling the ears, paws, muzzle, collar area, and rear end often provokes a defensive reaction in an adult dog if these areas have not been desensitized during puppy hood. Similarly, an adult dog may act fearfully or defensively when you stare into his eyes, if as a puppy he was not taught to enjoy direct eye contact. Some areas become sensitive over time simply because nobody bothers to examine them. For example, few owners regularly inspect their dog's rear end, or open his mouth to examine the teeth. Some areas are naturally sensitive and may provoke a reaction even in puppies. For example, nearly every puppy will bite your hand if you firmly take hold of his leg or paw. Other areas become sensitive because of bad husbandry and mishandling. Dogs with hangy-down ears, which are prone to infection, soon come to associate ear examinations with pain. Similarly, many adult dogs associate being stared at or being grabbed by the collar with bad times. Dogs quickly become hand-shy when people take them by the collar to lead them to confinement, grab them by the collar to put them on leash (ending an otherwise enjoyable play session in the park).

Guarding Valued Objects

Object-guarding, a common problem with family dogs, will develop throughout puppy hood if owners allow it to. Owners may fail to notice their adolescent dog becoming increasingly possessive and protective. Some may actually encourage their puppy's protective displays, thinking they are cute. It is natural for dogs to protect their possessions. In the wild, a wolf would hardly pop next door to borrow a cup of bones. Domestic dogs quickly learn that once something is gone, it is gone. So it is not surprising to find dogs trying to keep their possessions away from people.

If you frequently take food or toys away from your puppy and she never gets them back, your pup will learn that relinquishing an object likely means she will never see it again. Understandably, your pup might develop behaviours to keep objects away from you. She may run and hide with the object, hold on tight with her jaws, growl, snarl, and maybe snap. If you find you are backing down when your puppy is protecting any object, and are at a loss for what to do, seek help from a Certified Pet Dog Trainer immediately.

Basically, you have to teach your puppy that voluntarily relinquishing an object does not mean losing it for good. Your puppy should learn that giving up meals, bones, toys, and tissues means receiving something better in return—praise and treats—and also later getting back the original object.

As your puppy is eating dry kibble from her bowl, quickly put your hand in the bowl and offer a tasty treat. Give your puppy time to reinvestigate the dry kibble, to check for more treats, and to recommence eating. Then plunge your hand in the bowl and offer another treat. Repeat the procedure several times. Your pup will soon become accustomed and look forward to sudden hand movements around her food bowl. This exercise impresses puppies to no end.

Thank you for using my puppy course to train your puppy, keep up the training, this is just the beginning.

Enjoy your new puppy.

Many thanks

Sarah Maisey
Dog-trainer.co

Printed in Poland
by Amazon Fulfillment
Poland Sp. z o.o., Wrocław